M000033070

DON'T
READ THESE
POEMS
ALOUD

DON'T READ THESE POEMS ALOUD

CHEYENNE MARCELUS

Copyright © 2022 by Cheyenne Marcelus

All rights reserved. No part of this book may be reproduced or used in any manner without written permission except for the use of quotations in a book review. For more information, address: info@cheyennemarcelus.com

First Edition, 2022

ISBN 978-1-7779438-0-6 (paperback)
ISBN 978-1-7779438-1-3 (ebook)

www.cheyennemarcelus.com

—

Other works by Cheyenne Marcelus:

Good to Me: A Poetic Journey to Self-Preservation and Self-Acceptance

For *Micah*

I never tell my secrets;
I stuff them into poems and call them
metaphors.
I don't confront painful memories;
I craft them
into verses with cryptic titles.

I always tell the truth
but never without distraction.
Don't read these poems aloud,
but gaze at them with the silence of your own
unsaid truths.

CONTENTS

1

2

5

1

If I am honest

I'm always a bridge way from the *Welcome to Vicksburg*
sign;
a soap dish from summer,
drinking from a water hose and
skipping to a snowball stand;

two cups of sugar shy of Kool-Aid
or a buttered biscuit away from matriarchy,
three Betty Wright choruses from barefoot and pregnant;

an auntie away from eleven cousins,
a Piggly Wiggly coupon shy of a
road Trip to Louisiana,
seventeen miles from the smell of cow manure;

a pair of ripped pantyhose shy of a seven-night revival
and, quite frankly, I could use some deliverance;
sanctity from the sins I've accumulated north of the Mason-
Dixon,
a country-ass creek water baptism to cleanse me
and calamine to ease the itch.

If I've done the math correctly
I'm only forty summers shy of a burial in my grandmother's
backyard,
          and I need to make it home in time.

Fear

We met when I was 6
curled against a wall;
my feet heavy beneath me,
my knees wet with tears.

You had me surrounded.

We've since had chance encounters
where you approach me from behind
and cover my eyes and with your hands;
moments where you steal my breath and leave me frozen.
Remember me?

And now you're here
hovering over my bed
threatening to suffocate me.
You'll die before I let you rest.
You'll always succumb to me.

I wrestle with you

and this time
I am fighting for my life;
your hands tight around my neck,
your knee firm against my womb.
I dig my thumbs into your eyes;
I am tired of you seeing me this way.
You begin to falter,
and I drive my forearm to your throat and silence you;
this is my best defense.
Your grip loses its splinter
and I am free to bury you.

These ghosts won't let me forget

I've got to stop being so friendly with these ghosts;
I let them call me out of class and take me to the playground
of an apartment complex I haven't lived in since I was eight;
it's no wonder they take advantage.

I go to sleep and wake up in 2005
kicking a hole in my closet door
because *dammit I don't want to wear the pantyhose!*

I'm cha-cha slidin' at my wedding reception and before the
song ends
I'm riding shotgun over the bridge to New Orleans,
my press-and-curl waving from the window of my
grandmother's red Neon.

I may be washing dishes and end up in front of a powder
pink dollhouse,
arranging Barbie's in the living room like Destiny's Child in
the *Say My Name* video.

These ghosts are harmless at first;
we take these idle trips through innocuous memories
and they might fool me into thinking they're only nostalgic;

then the yelling starts.
There's a running shower and two bedroom doors between us
but I can hear it.

I can't sleep so I run
and these ghosts follow me back to my late twenties
to remind me that not a whole lot has changed.

When I disagree,

they show me mirror memories
from three and thirteen years ago.
Those nights I hear swear words in my sleep
and wake to the sound of breaking windows.

On my way to the bathroom, we detour to elementary school
where I am anxious and exhausted,
and being asked why I didn't sleep the night before.

The ghosts begin to gloat,
and before I can protest
I'm 19 driving to my grandmother's house at 2am
or 27 threatening not to come home again.

I love home, of course,
but it is a breeding ground for ghosts.
Every other visit they stuff themselves into my luggage
and hide in the seams of t-shirts and underwear;

and when the night terrors return,
the ghosts are there
offering to comfort me.

All the weapons in my Afro

I'm at the airport and I've been chosen
for the infamous Afro search,
the great despotic pat-pat up and through and over me;

I hope they don't find my spell book;
I hope my gris-gris doesn't fall to the floor and spill.

I hope they don't find the maps or the photographs,
the recipes or the cane sugar,
deshelled black-eyed peas or the rigid parts of collard greens.

I'm holding my breath hoping the TSA agent won't find the
airbrushed
rest in heaven t-shirt or the bones or the bullets;
not literal bullets, more like wooden beads and song lyrics,
aluminum foil and hot grits.

I hope the vinegar won't spill;
I worry that the Cognac might reveal itself or that the agent
will recognize
the smell of Fabuloso,

but I doubt it.

Ink therapy

inspired by a neck tattoo

They look frightening
like art;
punctured canvases and
half crumbled sculptures.
If you look too closely
you won't recognize them;
look away too quickly
and you won't see them at all.
It is a delicate gaze;
first at the sharpness of the brow bone
then at the symmetry of the jawline,
and finally,
the strength of the neck
softened by cherry red lips.
Who kissed him there?

Homegrown scribbles that look
green against their copper skin;
barbed wire collages
rendering images of unrequited freedom;
teardrops of loss and kindness
and the hardness that follows,
blood spilled like raspberries
turned from red to black
then scraped against the bone marrow;
a pain so deep,
a healing so permanent;
never to be erased,
forever admired
or abhorred,
enduring all the same.

This is what kills us

Our threshold for pain increases significantly
when we are more afraid of vulnerability than hurt.
We don't scream when we don't want others to hear.
The grimace on our face softens
when we wish not to appear weak;
hiding in plain sight,
tucking bruises between our toes,
letting the light illuminate only a facade of joy;
a desert mirage that fades at the touch.

But alone
we are revisited by the shrieks and shame;
the pain returns ten-fold
and we mourn until we are breathless.
Our legs give out beneath us
and our spines go limp;
the body retaliates from earlier being held taut.
Now it wheezes for pain like a life source;
as if agony were sustenance;
the contrast between the strong, impenetrable wall we present
and this now crumbling edifice.
Alone there is nowhere to hide,
no one to conceal ourselves from;
only the reality of the present hurt
staring us in the face
like the barrel of a gun.

2

Ask yourself

Everything burning inside a body eventually erupts;
sexual desire,
rage,
joy.

Everything spills out hotter than it enters.

Every criticism spills out the body
like daggers,

every hug like cotton candy.

What is put into a body
can only multiply,
mix with water,
and wildly regurgitate itself.

Every kind word,
every kiss or stroke
the body repays with wetness
and steam.

Every act of violence
or negligence
the body repays with salt water and iron.

The body pays its debts,
and reminds itself whom it owes.

It doesn't forget or
turn the other cheek.

It thuds and pants at the
sight of a violent memory,
reacts suddenly to the smell of fire
or the texture of wood.

It recognizes touch and chill,
rising itself to receive
or repel.

The body is more than a receptacle;
a lowly conduit we are just
passing through.

No, the body is a boomerang
and it always becomes itself.

Ask yourself:

What is a body;
a vessel
or a volcano?

Shelter

I can sometimes convince myself that the doors aren't
unhinged,
the light fixtures are made of crystal,
and there is sapphire beneath these rickety floorboards.

Every now and then,
when the Sun pierces through the shattered window
and tiger-stripes your face,
I remember what it's like to trust you.

Here and there,
I recall the cinnamon-scented candle
that sweetened the lies
I told myself about how the fire began.

Better now

I'm sifting through my lipsticks
wondering which one will make you hear me best;
Cherry Blossom,
Teddy Bare,
Sin.
(Somehow I always choose the gloss.)

I'm pondering my hair like a multiple-choice question;
A for Blowout
B for Bun
C for Afro.
Lately I've been throwing an old twist out in a pineapple and
that seems to keep you from looking past me.

I'm always wondering how to present myself to you;
timeless black dress,
girl next-door jeans and t-shirt,
seductive form-fitting miniskirt.
Which illusion might you prefer today?

Trying to be your fantasy is exhausting
but I've come too far to give up now.
I'm vanishing fast but surely there are still parts of me
left to give;
an arm,
a leg,
the right side of my brain.
What must be castrated
before I become your picture-perfect dream of a girl?

Here I am stressing over lipstick
when it's my mouth you want;
a choir orifice singing your praises

———

and whistling to the tap of your foot.
I'm fiddling with my hair
when you want everything underneath;
scalp and scalpel;
emptied through.

There I'll be;
your picture-perfect puppet of a woman,
recreated in the image of your *preferences.*
I can be good to you this way,
never mind how I'll be to me.
I am merely a vessel
for your idea of perfection.

Rearrange me.
Incise my breasts,
remove the heart;
plump and lift.
Cinch the waist
until there is no room for the ribs.
Extend the legs,
shorten the feet.
Lengthen the lashes,
and close the eyes.
Remove all the insides.
Insert yourself.

Better now?

Innocent girl

She knits a pink scarf
to tie around her mouth
so her screams are filtered through temperance.

She recounts the story teary-eyed,
cups her hands together like a Catholic choir soprano
as she fearfully identifies her attacker.

She lands
facedown,
palms planted near her ears;
tastes blood and
pretends its strawberry.
She rises to flee,
but does not rise to fight.

Instead she lays herself at the mercy of spectators who,
if she lies there feeble enough,
      if her whimper is poignant enough,
           if she has always been kind
                and never beneath reproach,
will believe that she is worthy of believing,
and perhaps even protecting.
They may lift her atop their moral high grounds
and proclaim
This one is undeserving of abuse.

She uses lipstick and clay
to build bridges to sanctuary.
She washes her hands with perfume
in hopes that purity may be her refuge.
She knows she must appear blameless and docile;
and strength is a stain

like blood on a lamb;
and lambs must be without blemish;
unprovocative.
Don't give the wolf a reason.

She knows victims must be without question;
and women who fight back leave too much to the
imagination.
If she can strike back,
perhaps she can strike first.
The mere possibility is threatening
and does not inspire compassion,
but admonishment.

So then it must be safer to lie beneath the whip
than to rise at the stake;
the former may bruise and welt
but the latter will surely burn.

Hwy 6

She grips me tightly; palms wet, pulse raging.
She squeezes her eyes shut for a moment too long. *Look up
or we'll crash!*
She looks forward and I notice   the bruise underneath
her eye,   the scratch on her neck,   the blood on her
collar.

We won't be seeing him again.

tap tap

I took the afternoon appointment.
I had classes that morning so it seemed -
reasonable.

I took the scenic route.
The Sun hugged the trees in a way that made me feel
almost safe.

But I wasn't late;
seven minutes early dressed in a pale pink chiffon blouse,
hair strategically placed to conceal my neck -
presentable.

I took each curious step
consciously paced;
a sort of fearful two-step.

tap tap
went the sandy colored oxfords
up the ridged staircase,
down the glassy hallway,

knock knock
on the cherry wood door,
quaintly and not judicially.
I'm only here to say what happened
I thought.

I don't remember the sound of *come in*,
or whether she rose from her fiery cathedra
or wafted me towards my seat like a fly.

---

tap tap
went the pen.
I spoke eloquently
but not without emotion.

tick tock
went the clock.
I spoke concisely
but not withholding detail.

tap tap
went the pen.
Her eyes never rose to meet me;
bewitched by the story on the page in front of her,
until

How did his shirt rip?

tick -

tap -

Her breath melted my face.
Well when I   got up from the floor,
I -

tap tap
went the pen.
Many have said the two of you had a volatile relationship.

Yes, but
I didn't -

TAP! TAP!
went the pen,
and then I saw the eyes;

———

frigid blue irises met with charcoal pupils,
furrowed eyelids adorned with ashen.

I don't like girls like you
they hissed toward me,

and it occurred to me that the Old Mistress had a preference;
and I should have taken the morning appointment.

3

A whistle through the pews

Hot-mouthed in a barley field,
I whisper *holy* and a fire runs
up the hill towards the dogwood tree.
Can you hear me now? I yell.

I stay until night
and greet the Moon with pleasantries.
When she asks what troubles me
I tell her everything is a woman.

The grass between my toes and the
gasoline beneath my tongue
is a woman who feels deserted;
she destroys herself to spite her Creator.

The wariness in my gut and the
raw spots on my heel
is a woman afraid to ask why;
she falls on her face and
begs for forgiveness.

Before the fire reaches the pews,
the stained-glass window is a woman
who asks if I am sure.
The fire ceases, as it always seems to
and I tell her
of course not.
Hallelujah, nothing is for sure.

A riot is a storm

a blade splintered in the kneecap
and still-falling rain
hailstone teardrops pounding a tin roof
I hear them dying outside

the wind is a siren
and thunder beats against the skull
then tells the brain to steady itself or else

lightning strikes an orifice in the pavement
and blames the puddle for its blood.

Fire

I lie in fetal position
against the earth I birthed;
I exchange kisses with the Sun
and let the wind whisper apologies to me,
I feel blades of grass like daggers against my back
like a thousand daggers.

I see sons return to soil
long before the planting season,
see them fall like leaves
from the lynching tree
and shatter in my palms.

I see daughters plucked from innocence
like daisies in mid bloom,
withered like scorched raisins;
ripened then devoured.

I mourn like thunder;
this earth I birthed betrays me.
I have given you light,
I've clothed your gardens with my hair,
I've carved mountaintops between my shoulder blades,
I've given you harvest and spring water;

perhaps,
I should give you
fire.

Cadaver

Apparently, I am good
at being in uncomfortable situations.

When needles danced
across my back
I sat anchored to a chair
humming to the buzz of the cartridge.

When saline pierced
through my wrists
I *did so well*
at shadowing the fear and loneliness
traveling up my spine.

When changing railroad tracks
scurried past my ears
I lay frozen;
wedged into myself until the crossing bell rang.
I was so still.

Kind of makes me wonder:

For what was I made?

To sit frigid and punctured
and fondled about;

to have blood drained from me
like cane sugar harvest;

to be looked over with confusion
and carelessness,
and be told *maybe it's just your -*

Are you sure you -

Probably gonna be a while -

You'll need to talk to your -

Hope you feel better -

I've decided to always report upwards
on pain scales.
I tell other brown-bodied women to do the same.

I've read too many stories,
too many personal essays.
I tell my husband he *must* advocate for me
if I am near death or inexplicable pain.
Threaten to sue or call the news.
Don't be afraid to be the angry Black man
I say.

I wish there was a candle I could light,
a sure-fire sage I could burn
a spell or ritual
for every pregnancy announcement,
hospital admittance,
routine visit,
clinical trial
of every ailing or jubilant Black woman;

something I could do,
some way to be sure.

If the body be a deity

then She is not to be worshipped,
but to be honored.

Her Living Word is breath;
sped up and slowed down,
panting in pleasure,
sighing in despair.

The gut is Her tabernacle,
and intuition gives a sermon
on rest and boundaries.

She has few commandments
save for kindness and attunement;
practices little religion
save for dance and desire.

She asks not to be denied
or suppressed or made an apology.
She demands love,
in whole, and not in part.

If the body be a deity,
there be no promised land;
only cell and tissue,
fat and skin,
color, scars,
and Blood;

Her precious Blood.

Black female bodies

I once did a Google search for images of "Black girls having fun".
I instead found images of Black girls gone missing.
2 Black girls gone missing from campus
    2 Black girls gone missing from church
        2 Black girls gone missing from a playground
           2 Black girls gone missing from DC
              2 Black girls gone missing
              from Chicago
and to disconnect the missing from the discovered,
2 Black female bodies
they would often phrase it.

Sometimes one body may have collapsed a few feet away
from the other
and they would be presented as separate unrelated incidents;
as if they were not near to one another,
tethered together by cracked bones and dried blood;
dear to one another,
with families waking together
filling their bellies with similar contents of soul food;
as if their homegoings wouldn't be at the same missionary
Baptist,
sermoned by the same pastor who is exhausted of funerals.

2 Black female bodies;
the missing girls who were missing too long.
If there were really such strength in numbers
they'd call out to each other
and ascend their way home.
If I avoided the footsteps of all the missing Black girls
I'd have nowhere to step,

Nowhere to play,   nowhere to pray,   no school to
attend,   no babysitter,   no boyfriend,
    no best friends,
       Nowhere to eat, sleep, or shit.

And they never give enough detail
about the soul that has left the Black female body.
They don't show the communities mourn;
they don't capture the emptiness of her former classrooms
and hallways,
or show a montage of the doodles in her notebooks,
a neighbor on the news saying she was such a sweet child
or a spirited child,
but nonetheless a child;
connecting her to someone's womb.

I don't think a decade from now there will be a documentary
about each of the missing Black girls
who were Resurrected as Black female bodies.
No, there may instead make one big documentary
about the epidemic of Black girls gone missing between this
year to that year
and how nobody really knew
and we only read news of it in Instagram comments;
perhaps a single docuseries where a handful of the country
full of Black female bodies receive souls and names.
I don't know which of them will truly get to rest.
I can't say for sure what God may greet them.
So many missing Black girls
become Black female bodies;
who knows what the bodies become.

In reverence to the exiled Queen

Bitter Earth,
I dig a staff into your face
and proclaim
This land belongs to the Queen.
You don't have to bow to her
but the truth will bring you to heel.

She is the legacy of those who hand stitched the soil,
whose howls in the night orchestrated the wind.
She is of the wombs
who bore the grass
and spit spring water from their breasts.

Her father's blood ascended to sunshine
and his skin blanketed the night's sky.
His limbs fashioned the trees,
and she is of the branches.
She belongs to the generation of wildfires
that sear through whips and chains.

A throne of melted crowbars and sapphire,
awaits her return;
a crown of bones and brass
curses her detractors.
Even now,
the Blood of her soldiers seeps through the floorboards;

She will be back for her kingdom.

4

Bride

She cloths herself in motifs from her grandmother's
tablecloth,
hand stitched and beaded through November weeds.
She drapes her neck with seeds from the harvest
and places the blooms atop her head.
She moves down an aisle of magnolia leaves and
honeysuckle.

A dark figure awaiting her
stands eerily beneath a barbwire arch;
a caged dove to his right,
Bible to his left.
Towards her he extends a blood-spattered palm.
A voice descends from the sky
          Do you take this man?

She grasps his hand
and disintegrates.

Where are you now?

Perhaps on the cusp of some pesky illusion,
a ways away from laughter and disappointment

A roundabout from *I told you so*
crafting a joke of self-discovery

Crouching forward whispering adages
into a clogged drain, moments before sewer explodes on my
face

Somewhere between a crack in a windshield
and a traveling itch

A rolling boil beneath the ash,
waiting to erupt.

A trauma bond comes undone

I wonder if you feel us   unfolding;
tearing at the seal,   fibers
opening themselves like butterfly wings.

Wonder if you've noticed the skin around the
scab   darkening;
a rustic purple ring around a tie-dye middle,   artfully
disappearing itself.

My body is starting to forget   the feeling
of walking on stilts holding hands   with you.
I am beginning to unlearn the balancing act;

I gave someone a hug yesterday   with no regard
for the teacup atop my head   and now
I couldn't feel farther from you.

Your voice sounds like the crackling of coal   being
whispered on
and that is not how I remember it.   I chastise myself
for feeling resentful.

This is a new kind of pain,   like moments
before wax dries   and when it does,
what on earth will I do with myself?

I'm sorry and I'd like to come home

How do I begin to apologize to myself
for not being present in my body?

> I'm sorry you have spilled
> yourself to fulfill my
> fleeting desires.
> It's not your fault
> the shadows in my gut
> eat away at any measure of satisfaction.

> I see you there and I
> wish to join you,
> but there are rocks in my
> pockets and I fear
> I'll lose the fight with the current.

> Brittle and prickly pillows and
> satin dresses line an alter
> I dreamt about for months,
> and now I am the runaway bride.

> I'm sorry I made you beg
> and chase fireflies
> through concrete valleys,
> digging up soil with raw fingertips
> just for me to bury myself.

Is there something I can give you
to make up for lost time;
a sort of tithe
or sacrament?

I'd offer you the fat of an ox
but I'm afraid it's grown
thin and undesirable.

The lace around my garments
is disheveled and
all but ruined,

but I still have time, perhaps
to rock back and forth in space
with you.

Maybe I'll find solstice,
a sweet spot
on the cusp of your girdle.

I might find new beauty
in you,
and you, in me.

Together, we might find fortress once more.

Ill-fitted love affair

I've tried it on a million ways from Sunday,
and still it hangs off the shoulder and clings to the belly.

I've added belts and buttons
and shortened the hem.

Between dry-cleaning and steaming, I am all wrung out;
all out of room to grow, with no space for compromise.

It fits too tight and flows too heavy.
It's too long around the arms and clingy
near the neck.

The bust is smothered and the hips are confined;
I'm gasping when I sit and tripping as I walk.

I've had enough of shape shifting and girdling myself
into this outside woman.

This looks nothing like the pictures.

This is a garden

This
      Body
            ain't
                         no
dumping ground.

You can't
toss your nonrecyclables onto me
then come again next week.

You can't
dangle your scraps   over my face
and expect me to swallow;
        stuff me with your spoils
           and watch effluent run down my legs.

I am not a house for your undesirable things.

      And anyway,
           I've decided to grow a garden
and you keep mucking up my soil.

Turnips to the right,
tomatoes and sweet peppers to the left;
gonna line the edges with marigolds -

           You'll need to move that old sofa you dumped
out here.
           Gotta make room for my potatoes;
               they'll need lots of space, you know.

      Oh, and grab those tattered clothes you left near the
fence.

56

I'm going to plant a hydrangea bush there.

Yeah,
This
        Body
                ain't
                        no
dumping ground.

        This is a garden.
    You best be on your way now.
            Take care.

Love was/ Love
is

I was 12 years old writing about love.
I felt I understood that it may be difficult
and heartbreaking,
but I would always have a desire for it.

I remember feeling like love was provocative;
that it made you angry and irrational.
I saw people abuse those they loved.
I cut the stuffing out of a teddy bear because love made me
jealous;
I thought it normal to be burned by such a fiery emotion.
I thought it appropriate to chase after it
and hit a wall instead.

I have since learned love
is vulnerability;
a wide-open scab in a saltwater bath,
equal parts stupidity and fearlessness.
It's running hand in hand to the edge of a cliff
where you'll either jump or fall;
either way you'll fly for a little while.
You'll be lighter,
having given parts of you to someone else;
you'll be heavier
having carried them for some time.
You'll be exhausted
and energized,
drained and full.
Love is the great dichotomy you work and play to
understand;
give and take,

listen and yell,
move and be still.
It requires so much
and yet so little.

Although it is hard,
it is not unhealthy.
It's uncomfortable,
maybe even risky,
but it won't put you in danger.
It's asks much of you,
but it won't kill you.
It won't make you hate yourself.
It will chase you back.
It will want for you
and hurt for you
and give itself to you fully.
It is not one sided;
it is as patient and long suffering as you are,
it is as kind as you are.
It will not burn you to death,
but ignite you to diamonds instead.

On intimacy

Why do you confuse connection for intimacy;
bleeding yourself into every hand you shake,
shaving off pieces of your heart with every hug,
sharing your secrets with every passing hello?

Who was it that looked away from you
when they should have been looking after you?
Who shut the door
in the face your pain;
who didn't listen?

Who didn't see
or rather did not look?
Point me towards the emptiness.

Consider filling that space
in a way that does not leave you
bare and destitute;
having given your whole self
to those who only sent for half.

Let's talk about intimacy with one's self;
the armor of your own steady hand,
the warmth of your own arms
wrapped around your chest;
seeing your secrets
with no shame,

validating your own feelings.
Self -
Soothing
I believe it's called;
coddling yourself when you cry;

loving yourself with the lift of a thousand galaxies
then using that love as the measuring stick
for how others must love you.
It is, after all,
the measuring stick.
They will, after all,
only treat you as well as you treat yourself.

Find in you
what you look for in every passing stranger.
only then,
can you demand it from the world.

5

This is what saves us

There is nothing more delicate than the feeling of a tear
falling on your collarbone;
nothing more visceral than the tightness of the gut
reminding you that instinct can't be silenced;
the knot in the throat that hums you to sleep
or the under-eye puffiness that wakes you;
the seduction of telling the truth loud enough for others to
hear.

Freedom is calling it by name,
giving it a face and styling its hair;
lying beneath its body without resistance;
feeling the full weight of this iniquity
and deciding not to stand against it;
falling apart so that you may realize the wholeness of
vulnerability,
and rise in the arms of a friend.

Brownies

Only you can tell me my bra strap is showing
and make it sound like
I love you,

and when you ask me to repeat something that has been
overtaken by my undeniably Southern twang,
it sounds like
I'm glad I'm from where you're from.

Girl, shut the fuck up!
is a love letter to my wittiness
and I'm glad I can make you laugh.

You ate my mama's spaghetti knowing full well your ass was
allergic to mushroom,
and we can make a meal out of anything!
How did pickles, lettuce, and ranch become a salad?

I know Precious isn't supposed to be a comedy
but we reenact scenes and laugh 'til our sides hurt.

I like when you yell at me for having long drunk
conversations with strangers.
Girl, come on!
sounds like
I'll always protect you.

I don't know about that
sounds like
I don't want you to get hurt.

You almost got slapped!
is an opportunity for me to recognize how I hurt you

and received the forgiveness I rarely deserve.
I appreciate that.

And when I say
Do I need to come over there?
it isn't a question;
it is a declaration of my compassion for you, friend.
I know that hurt
and I'll fuck a motherfucker up for you, friend.

We need to have drinks!
is code for
Let's dance and talk shit
and make another memory to cling to when we're 1000 miles
apart again.

And when I say you ain't shit
I'm really just admiring your growth.
You're resilient, friend
and I appreciate you not leaving me behind.

How you doin'?
is really
How you doin'?
and I mean it every time.

I want to know the truth every time.
What you doing?
is a greeting.
How you doin'?
is a call to action;
Take care of yourself, friend,
and I'm always here to help.

—

65

Happy for real

When's the last time you were real happy
like

laughing loud in public happy
running around outside barefoot and nappy-headed happy

like watermelon that you can't eat inside happy
Quit running in and out! Stay in the yard! happy?

When's the last time you were fish fry happy
Jig-a-low   jig   jig   a low happy
last night of vacation bible school happy

snowball with the ice cream happy
toe touches on a trampoline happy

I'm cooking red beans and rice today happy
Please ma, can I stay? happy

a pickle from the penny lady happy
a brown paper bag full of candy happy

beads with the foil at the ends happy
My cousins be my best friends happy

riding bikes in the sun happy
passing notes just for fun happy

when's the last time you were done getting yo' hair combed
happy,
downloaded a new ringtone happy?

Ain't even know how good we had it,

Happy.

What song are you?

Strung through the saddle like satin
or like barbwire;
colliding across cilia
or screeching off walls;

smooth like jazz,
like a Manhattan,
like warm maple syrup;
freshly lotioned hands gliding across a lovers back

or bass like thunder,
roaring down pain and vengeance;
loudness like lightning
striking violently,
setting the ground ablaze;
a fire that grows and consumes
a trail of lovers burned alive?

A lullaby
or a drive by;

shouts and shrills singing praises
and professing lowliness,
are you like gospel;
hands high
hip low
Shake the devil off
round through the pews,
grabbing of hands,
latching together of loved ones;
a community at the altar
bowed before the throne of togetherness?

Are you a dying genre
of fatherless kids
rocked to bed by Styrofoam cups
filled with lava
passed from mouth to rhythm
a clever arrangement of obscenities;
destructive words brilliantly sequenced;
a chorus of detrimental catch phrases?

The ornaments fall from the alter with each syllable;
a mother unfastens with the lash of each derogatory lyric,
like a whip across her womb.

Legacy

I hope I give
you something
you need,
not that I wish
you to be
voided;
but if a void
exists,
I hope I give
you something
that fills you.

I hope there is
something about
me that heals
you.
I hope that I am
not just here
existing among
you;
I hope our
encounters
aren't so
superficial.
I hope I touch
you deep;
that some dance
I dance
resonates.
I hope I leave
my fingerprints
on your soul.

I don't want to be doing
this only for my accord.
I can be selfish at times,
yes, but I am giving at
my core.
I hope that in all my
giving that you receive
some reward; maybe
the Sun peaking
through a cloud,
a cool breeze in a too
warm room,
a ladder,
an open door,
a house with no ceiling.
I hope I give you
something you've
hoped for.

I hope I lighten the
load,
not that I wish for you
to be burdened;
however if there is a burden
I hope to carry it at least some of the way up.
I hope I shoulder enough to make a difference;
so your back is strong and your knees withstand the climb.
I hope it is more than self-serving pleasantries I leave behind.

Whatever I leave
behind, I hope it falls
below and lifts you, like
a parachute;
like a fighter jet;
like an angel.

I hope it lifts you out of
doubt,
depression,
or writer's block;
or whatever funk makes
you feel
not quite good enough,
not quite whole enough;
imperfect,
unready,
undeserving,
unworthy.
I hope I leave behind a
match, so you can set
that shit on fire.
In terms of legacy, that
is my desire.

An ode to Beyoncé's accent

I appreciate Beyoncé's accent;

not in "Halo" or "Ave Maria",
but in *people don't make albums anymore* and the *Tex-is* at
the beginning of "Daddy Lessons".

I like the way she says *mama*
and the gracefulness of the habitual "be"
in *I hear you be the block, but I'm the lights that keep the
streets on.*

To me her drawl sounds like a sewing machine
threading country-Black and excellence
seamlessly like the runs in "Countdown".

I like all the places her Southern accent has been,
positioning itself atop the Queen's English and the master's
enunciation
looking down on them from a throne of golden leotards
saying
Ain't God good.

Galactica

I am no more salt than I am cane sugar,
no more soil than coal,
but I am all things
combusting at the edge of an envelope
filled with amethyst and Sulphur.
If ever there was a box
it was inconceivably large and impossible to fill.

Lately I've been leaning in
to the questions
and there is not edge enough to fall through
this strong tower of genomes
and histories
and fibers
and stories
and etchings
and lead
and ink.

Somewhere on the other side of Mars
my right-hand drafts apologies to the moments
when I remembered to shrink myself
into abridgments
so that hiring managers
and healthcare providers
and new acquaintances
could better understand the breadth and depth of God.

I am, of course, god.
She and I are one
and so many other things simultaneously;
no more deity than identity,
no more religion than relationship.

If ever there was a hell,
it was meant by living
a halfway life.

It is, I think,
the greatest betrayal of God
to deny oneself of being
all of oneself.

Bloodline

Thick off-white petals feel
like twice-threaded silk.
If you could pry the leaves
apart from themselves,
you might find blood in the in-between.

i.
A girl is born to a
woman with a grandmother whose
hair is endlessly Black and sweeping,
whose cheekbones stand high and
spread at the sound of the rooster's caw.
The red wooden house with the fig tree in front
holds bronze photos of a late prophet
who took root across the river.

ii.
The river has blood on either side
and the bridge is a hearse.
Sandy beaches are cemeteries
and every new customer at the girl's first job
tells her they knew her father.
She rolls these excerpts into silverware
napkins
and leaves them at the foot of a sunset
too bright to behold.

iii.
Her mother weds the man with
the golden smile

———

and the brown Grand Marquis.
He takes her down a gravel
lane to a garden with no end,
where she is held by a slender
woman
whose hands are soil and
plough;
whose heart, much like his,
has room enough for a rose of
another name.

iv.
Of this, she quilts a
complicated tapestry
whose colors are wild
and mystifying,
but the thread is strong
and it warms her on
cold, rigid nights.
It reveals her like a
mirror
and she is proud and
sure.

v.
On an almost
perfect
September
evening,
she dances with
a man who, too,
has a father
among the
stars.

Two of her three
grandmothers
wave them off
with long
steamed
sparklers
whose heads
they bury in the
sand.
Together they
find ground that
lifts beneath
them
and folds itself
into suitcases.

vi.
Months later, he holds her
shoulders
as her spine vomits towards her
gut.
The slender woman whose
heart
had room enough for a rose of
another name
has withered fast and violently
from her liver.
They are to wear light blue
instead of black,
and she will be carried in an
urn of soil and plough
instead of a casket.

vii.
During a winter milder than the one before,
the tapestry bleeds itself and a boy
with a face strikingly similar to hers
pulls the girl up from drowning,
and keeps her warm on cold, rigid nights.

viii.
His eyes are brown and piercing;
his face glows with joy as though he is often visited
by the fathers and grandmothers of his parents.
He sees the blood in the magnolia,
he tastes the grit of the river.
He sees and tastes and knows
for sure and for always
that he is loved.

Mother Tongue

My mother tongue is at the
mouth of the Mississippi and
she sings the blues and spews
blessing oil. 102 miles north
of the coast she grows
collards and turnips. She
rears six chickens and a
rooster. She is an
entrepreneur with a husband
who pays the bills. Her
money is for the grandkids,
the collection plate, and the
biweekly press-and- curl.

My mother tongue has a
drawl. Like *y'all* and *finna*
and *ain't God good*. Ain't she
beautiful. She is nurturing
and steadfast and don't take
no shit. She soaks her beans
the night before and there is
no such thing as unsweetened
tea. She doesn't sit her purse
on the floor. She doesn't
spare the rod. She doesn't
miss a Sunday.

My mother tongue is the
sound of fresh flowers and
neatly folded napkins, honey
baked ham adorned with
pineapples, five inch heels
and coffee-colored
pantyhose. She is soprano on
Sunday and alto on Monday.
She sings blessings or curses
according to the occasion.
She yells *PUSH!* or
Hallelujah! or *Don't shoot!*
according to the occasion.

My mother tongue resounds.
From Mississippi to
Chicago, she resounds.
From generation to
generation, she resounds.
She is Harriet, and Fannie,
and Sarah, and Nina. She is
Ruth, and Gussie, and
Dorothy, and Jeannie, and
Barbra. She is my mother
today and my daughter
tomorrow. I whisper her
name and shatter a
mountain.

Acknowledgements

Grateful acknowledgements to the publications that featured earlier versions of the following poems:
"All the weapons in my Afro" and "Happy for real", *805 lit+art*
"Mother Tongue" and "Black female bodies", *Penumbra Online*
"What song are you?", *Eve Poetry*

Grateful acknowledgements to my loved ones who have read earlier versions of these poems and provided invaluable feedback. I am forever grateful for the many ways you all love, support, and correct me.

DISCUSSION QUESTIONS

Discussion Questions

1. The concepts of "home" and "homesickness" are referenced throughout *Don't Read These Poems Aloud.* What does it mean to miss home? How do we reconcile homesickness with the decision not to live where we are from? What are some ways we create a "home away from home"?

2. How would you answer the question posed in the poem "Ask yourself"? - Is the body and vessel or a volcano? What are the implications of either answer? How do we treat our bodies accordingly?

3. Think of the following lines from the poem "Better now".

There I'll be;
your picture-perfect puppet of a woman,
recreated in the image of your *preferences*.

What are the dangers of transforming oneself
to fit the preferences of another? Think of this
not only in a romantic context, but also in
familial, friendly, or professional
relationships. Is change sometimes necessary?
How do we draw the line between good and
necessary change versus harmful self-
degradation?

4. Think of the poem "Innocent girl". What do
   you feel is the extent of the progress we've
   made in believing victims of abuse? Does this
   differ for victims who are women, Black, or
   LGBTQIA+? What are some markers of
   progress in this area?

5. In the poem "A whistle down the pews", a
   woman struggles with her understanding of
   God and religion. From your perspective,
   what is the conclusion of this poem? Where
   does she land in her quest to ask *why*?

---

6. Think about the poems "Black female bodies" and "Cadaver" regarding the mishandling of Black women's bodies in American society. What are tangible and immediate steps that should be taken to irradicate this systemic issue? How can we each play an active role in protecting Black women?

7. In the context of intimate partnerships, how do we communicate evolving boundaries; particularly enforcing boundaries that were not in place during earlier stages of the relationship? Do you believe the bounds of an existing romantic partnership can always be re-established or are there instances where it may be too late to evolve? For you, what makes a damaged relationship unsalvageable?

8. How has your perception of love changed with your life experiences? How do you define love? Have you become more or less hopeful towards romantic love with your lived experiences?

9. "brownies" and "This is what saves us" describe friendship as a saving grace. Do you feel we assign appropriate value to platonic friendships? What are some ways we can each show appreciation for the friendships in our lives?

10. Think of the defining elements of your culture. Now, think of the things that define who you are. How do these align? How apparent is the impact of your culture on who you are as an individual?

About the Author

Cheyenne Marcelus is a poet and performer from Columbia, Mississippi. Her work is heavily influenced by her Southern upbringing as well as her expatriate life in Canada. She is the author of Good to Me: A Poetic Journey to Self-Acceptance and Self-Preservation. Her work has appeared in Penumbra Online, Eve Poetry, Split This Rock, and the Centennial/19th Amendment issue of 805 lit+art. She resides in Ottawa, Ontario with her family. Visit **www.cheyennemarcelus.com** for more.

CPSIA information can be obtained
at www.ICGtesting.com
Printed in the USA
LVHW090031070222
710429LV00006B/336